RABBIT'S NEW FUR

A NATIVE AMERICAN TALE

retold by Richard C. Lawrence

illustrated by Matt Straub

MODERN CURRICULUM PRESS

Pearson Learning Group

Rabbit was clever. He liked to outwit the other animals. He especially liked to outwit any animal who got more attention than he did. And let's face it, just about every animal got more attention than Rabbit. Wolf, Bear, Fox, Snake, and Porcupine were all more dangerous than Rabbit. Skunk got noticed for his scent. Even Turtle, with his hard shell, his slow walk, and his wise eyes, got noticed more than Rabbit.

The other animals tolerated Rabbit, and he tolerated them. Sometimes he carried messages for them. He didn't like doing their chores, but he liked the chance to travel. He liked meeting new creatures he could outwit.

Once, the animals planned a dance to honor the creature with the most beautiful coat of fur. "Well, that's me," Rabbit thought, stroking his fur with glee. "When they tell me I've won, should I act surprised?"

But when the votes were in, Otter's fur was named most beautiful. Rabbit's job was to report the news to Otter. Rabbit was beside himself.

"How dare they?" he said to himself as he set off up the river to Otter's house. "They've ignored me once again. I'll get them for this with a vengeance. They'll see with whom they're dealing."

"I'll get them," Rabbit said. "I'll get that Otter. So he thinks he has the best fur, does he?"

The idea of vengeance made Rabbit run faster. He wouldn't have said anything if anyone could have heard him. He was a secretive little fellow.

Of course, when Otter opened his door, Rabbit acted as if he were Otter's biggest fan.

"I'm thrilled that I, a humble rabbit, have been chosen to invite you to a dance in honor of your beautiful fur."

Otter didn't know what Rabbit had on his mind.
He was glad he had been chosen. He was happy to
have Rabbit travel with him. And he was too polite to
ask questions like, "Weren't you outwitting a wolf the
last time I saw you?"

They set off down the river, and camped for the
night. They made a nice little fire. Otter caught a fish
and cooked it while Rabbit dined on dandelion greens.

"Vengeance will be mine," Rabbit vowed secretly.

As they were going to sleep, Rabbit said, "Uh-oh. I didn't realize it when I picked this campsite."

"What?" Otter asked.

"Maybe I should just ignore the stories they tell," Rabbit said, "but . . . ."

"What, what?" asked Otter in alarm.

"Well, they say that sometimes—not always, mind you—fire falls out of the sky here."

"Fire falls out of the sky?" Otter said, folding his furry forepaws over his head. "I've never heard of that."

"I've heard of it," Rabbit said.

"What have you heard?" asked Otter.

"Well, as I said, I don't think we should believe all the old myths. You know the kinds of things animals say."

"What do they say? What do they say?" Otter asked in bewilderment. "I live up the river. I don't hear about these things."

"Don't let it worry you," Rabbit said. He was smiling to himself.

"Here's what we'll do," Rabbit said. "Take off your fur and hang it in a tree. If any fire falls from the sky, the leaves and branches will protect it. Your fur won't have any holes burned in it. I'll sleep near it, to guard it. You sleep by the river. If fire falls from the sky, you can jump in the water."

"Good plan!" Otter said with gratitude. He felt lucky to have a friend like Rabbit. He took off his fur, hung it on a low branch, and went to sleep by the river.

While Otter slept, Rabbit picked up a big chunk of bark that had fallen from a tree. He scooped coals from the fire onto the bark. He flung the coals high into the air. Then he shouted, "Fire! Fire is falling from the sky!"

Otter woke up and saw the red embers falling through the air. He gave a shriek and jumped into the river in a panic.

Rabbit plucked Otter's fur from the tree and vanished.

Rabbit sprinted all the way down the river to the dance hall. He arrived just as the dance was about to begin.

He sneaked around to the back, and climbed into Otter's fur. He stuffed his fluffy tail in. He tied his long ears under his chin. He covered his nose and mouth with his paw. And he marched into the dance hall proudly, thinking, "I, Rabbit, have the most beautiful fur."

"Look. Is that Otter?" Possum called out, blinking because she couldn't see very well. "How lovely his fur looks tonight!"

"So there's our guest of honor," said Mink, who secretly thought he deserved the prize instead.

"Hooray!" shouted Bobcat, who reached out and tried to feel Otter's fur.

"Leave him alone. Give him room," said Bear, who was Otter's best friend.

Bear walked up to Otter—that is, to Rabbit—and shook his hand so hard, Rabbit almost cried.

CONGRATULATIONS OTTER!
The Most Beautiful Fur

"Glad you could make it here tonight," Bear said in his low, growly voice. "Your fur looks great. This couldn't happen to a nicer animal. Did you have any trouble getting here?"

"No, I got an early start," said Rabbit.

Rabbit danced all night, holding one hand over his face so no one would know who he really was.

"Otter, you look so secretive!" said Chipmunk when she danced with him.

"I'm not secretive," Rabbit said. "This is the newest dance."

Other animals began dancing with their hands in front of their faces too. No one else asked Rabbit about it.

But the young animals saw that something was not right. When Rabbit went outside to get some fresh air, the children followed him. They saw Rabbit tie his ears back under his chin. (His ears had come untied from all that dancing.) And they saw his rabbit face.

"That's not Otter!" said the fox kit.

"It's Rabbit trying to outwit us!" said the wolf whelp.

And the bear cub called out, "Look. It's Rabbit in Otter's fur!"

That brought Bear over, fast. Bear lifted Rabbit up in one huge paw and shook the Otter fur off him.

"What have you done with Otter?" he snarled. "If you've hurt my best friend, I'll take vengeance!"

"Please," Rabbit squeaked, "I don't know what you're talking about. I found this fur by the side of the river. Is it Otter's? I didn't know. I have no idea where Otter is. I certainly hope no harm has come to him. I myself will hunt down with a vengeance anyone who's hurt him!"

Bear gave a loud growl. "We've tolerated your tricks long enough. Go!"

Rabbit ran away.

"He thinks he can outwit Bear, does he?" Bear said. "Such tricks will not be tolerated while I'm here. I can tell you that."

"That's all very well, Bear," said Beaver, "but what about Otter? Shouldn't we send out a search party?"

The animals left a note for Otter, and spread out far and wide to look for him.

Bear found Otter a few minutes later. Otter was pale, wet, and shivering. He looked terrible without his fur. He looked a little bit like a rabbit.

"Rabbit told me something about fire falling from the sky," Otter moaned. "Then I saw it, and I jumped into the water just as he told me to. I don't know what happened to my fur. I've looked everywhere." Otter began to weep. "I'm sorry I spoiled the dance."

"You didn't spoil anything," Bear said. "It was Rabbit's doing. Now put your fur back on. You're cold and wet. Did you really jump into the river like this?"

"Yes, and guess what I did. I went swimming!"

Otter had never swum before, but from then on swimming was his favorite sport.

When Rabbit heard that he had actually helped Otter instead of outwitting him, he was angry. But he didn't say a word about it. For once, he was glad not to be noticed.

⊙ Comprehension Skill: Making Judgments

Modern Curriculum Press edition, 2004

ISBN 0-7652-3517-X

Printed in Mexico

6 16

Modern
Curriculum
Press
Pearson Learning Group

1-800-321-3106
www.pearsonlearning.com

Rabbit's New Fur: A Native American Tale

Power Reader #11

Comprehension Skill: Making Judgments

Genre: Folk Tale

DRA® Level	60
Guided Reading Level	W
Lexile® Measure	730L

1-800-321-3106
www.pearsonlearning.com

Modern
Curriculum
Press

Pearson Learning Group

ISBN 0-7652-3517-X

90000

9 780765 235176